Christmas
Program Builder
No. 58

LILLENAS
DRAMA

Christmas
Program Builder
No. 58

Compiled by
Kim Messer

KANSAS CITY, MO 64141

Copyright © 2005 by Lillenas Publishing Co. All rights reserved.

Scripture quotations marked (NIV) are taken from the *Holy Bible, New International Version*® (NIV®). Copyright © 1973, 1978, 1984 by International Bible Society. Used by permission of Zondervan Publishing House. All rights reserved.

Scripture quotations marked (KJV) are taken from the *Holy Bible,* King James Version.

Permission to make noncommercial photocopies of program builders is granted to the purchaser when three copies of the same book have been purchased. The photocopies cannot be sold, loaned, or given away.

Questions? Please write or call:
    Lillenas Publishing Company
    Drama Resources
    P. O. Box 419527
    Kansas City, MO 64114
    Phone: 816-931-1900 • Fax: 816-412-8390
    E-mail: drama@lillenas.com
    Web Site: www.lillenasdrama.com

Cover design: Michael Walsh

Contents

Preschool Recitations   7

Ages 5 to 7   9

Ages 8 to 10   11

Reading   12
   What Did Mary Know?   12

Poem   13
   The Perfect Part   13

Christmas Plays   15
   Mary and the Christ Child   15
   Conversations with Gabriella   21
   Secret Service   48

Preschool Recitations

Vigil

The Baby Jesus slept
As vigil Joseph kept.

                Mary Ann Green

Joy, Joy, Joy

Joy, joy, joy,
   Is what I want today.
I wish each one of you
   A joyful Christmas Day.

                Margaret Primrose

Angel Said

The angel said to Mary,
The Lord's child she would carry.

                Mary Ann Green

Christ's Glory

Again we hear the story
How Christ was born in glory
To bring us Peace and Love,
God's blessings from above.

                Dorothy Heibel

They Sang

The angels sang,
The shepherds came,
The star was bright
That Holy Night.

                Mary Ann Green

Jesus, Others, and You

CHILD 1: J stands for Jesus
         And also for joy.
CHILD 2: I'm glad that the Savior
         Was Mary's baby boy.
CHILD 3: O is for others.
CHILD 4: Taking time for their needs
         Makes us useful and
         happy.
CHILD 3: Yes, happy indeed!
CHILD 5: Y is for you.
ALL: We wish each of you
         A very Merry Christmas
         And a Happy New Year
         too.

                Margaret Primrose

Kings

The kings came from afar to
   worship Him.
They followed the star toward
   Bethlehem.

                Mary Ann Green

My Wish

Peace and joy
This Christmas morn.
That's my wish
For everyone.

                Robert Colbert

Rest

Rest, Baby, on the hay
For it is Your birthday.

           Mary Ann Green

When Jesus Came

Little Baby Jesus,
Who was born on Christmas Day,
Came to earth to save us
And take our sins away.

           Margaret Primrose

Ages 5 to 7

Follow the Star

(To be recited by three or more little kings.)
Cross the water,
Follow the star,
Travel the land
To a country so far.
We are going
To see the new king,
Born for all
Redemption to bring.

     Robert E. Snodgrass

I Thank You, Lord

I thank You, Lord, that Christmas
 joy
 Is something that will last.
I thank You that You'll stay in my
 heart
  When the holidays are past.

     Margaret Primrose

Adoration

Wise men came from faraway lands
To worship Christ the King.
May we, like them, our gifts of love
In humble adoration bring.

     Dorothy Heibel

What the Bells Say

When I hear the church bells ring,
 I can almost hear them sing,
"Come, come, come, and pray.
 Come thank the Lord for
  Christmas Day."

     Margaret Primrose

Wise Men

Wise men traveled many days
 Following Christ's star to greet
 Him.
Let us, like them, journey with hope
 That in our hearts we may seek
 Him.

     Dorothy Heibel

In Bethlehem

Ring aloud
The Christmas bells.
Listen to what they say.
Christ is born
In Bethlehem.
Welcome, happy day.

     Robert Colbert

Worship

...s in the heavens above
...ng of God's amazing love.
Shepherds in the fields below
Wonder at one star's bright glow.
So, may we, in worship and praise
Celebrate the Christ Child all our
    days.

Dorothy Heibel

Come to the Manger

Come to the manger;
    Come, kneel and pray.
Give thanks for the Baby
    Who was born Christmas Day.

He's the Lord of all
    And the King of Kings.
Come, share the joy
    That knowing Him brings.

Margaret Primrose

Decorating for Christmas

As we trim the Christmas tree
For the holiday season's start,
May we hold the Christ Child's love
Forever in our heart.

Dorothy Heibel

What Is Christmas?

(Make signs for each of the italicized words and have them revealed when the words are spoken.)

CHILD 1: Christmas is *peace*;
CHILD 2: Christmas is *love*.
CHILD 1, 2: Christmas is the *hope*
          God sends from above.
CHILD 3: Christmas is *joy*;
CHILD 4: Christmas is *glory*.
CHILD 3, 4: Christmas is hearing
          A wonderful *story*.
CHILD 5: Christ came from above
          With no wealth nor fame.
CHILD 6: He came as our Savior.
ALL: Praise His wonderful
          name!

Margaret Primrose

Ages 8 to 10

Precious Child

(Have a girl recite this at the manger.)
Precious Child in swaddling clothes,
You are the one the Master knows.
A special gift within a manger,
Friend to all and not a stranger.
Those who believe will not think it
　odd
That You are the only Son of God.

　　　　　　　Jean Conder Soule

Gifts for Everyone

I cannot buy a present
For every one of you,
But I have thought of something—
Something I can do.

I cannot package joy
Nor peace or hope or love,
For these are from the Father,
Who sends them from above.

But I can bow my head
And say a simple prayer.
Though it won't be long or loud,
I'll say it because I care.

Thank You, thank You, Jesus,
That You are here today.
Thank You, Heavenly Father
That You hear us when we pray.

Bless all of those who came
To celebrate Christ's birth.
We thank You, Lord and Savior,
For the day He came to earth.
Amen

　　　　　　　Margaret Primrose

Faith in the Savior

The great joy in all the earth
Was the news of the Savior's holy
　birth.
The greatest hope of the world
　today:
Jesus still lives and hears us pray.
If we have faith in the King of kings
We will know the joy the Savior
　brings.
By following His will and helping
　others
Peace and love will join all men as
　brothers.

　　　　　　　Dorothy Heibel

Reading

What Did Mary Know?

What did Mary know
   The night that He was born,
When she held Him in her arms
   Upon first Christmas morn?

What did Mary know
   When the shepherds came to call?
They knelt and worshiped Him,
   Filled with wonder, joy, and awe.

What did Mary know
   When the wise men traveled far,
Bringing such expensive gifts,
   Guided by just a star?

What did Mary know
   When in her heart she pondered,
As He taught and healed the people,
   While in His steps she wandered?

What did Mary know
   When her Son died on the cross?
As He looked down upon her,
   How could she bear the loss?

What did Mary know?
   She knew to trust in God;
That she would be His servant
   As she promised when He called.

                    Martha S. Campbell

Poem

The Perfect Part
by James D. Jueers

Auditions for the Christmas play are in the music room
Sally Johnson last year was a cow and had to "moo."
This year she hopes for something more than just a simple beast.
Perhaps an angel or Wise Man, Innkeeper's Wife at least.

She gets the part of Mary in the pageant offering.
For weeks the Johnsons hear the song that Sally soon will sing.
She only has a solo with a spoken line or two.
Determined now to do her best, she sings it till she's blue.

Rehearsals for the pageant all go off without a problem.
The words are learned by heart before Mrs. Toddy has to scold them.
Performance night arrives so soon, the crowd begins to sing,
The children in bright costumes stand quietly in the wings.

First comes the angel Gabriel, a seasoned actor, he,
With gesturing, proclaiming Mary soon will bear a King.
The old greedy Innkeeper firmly says he has no room.
The bright and shining angels sing their songs in perfect tune.

Sally's heart is pounding as she moves to center stage.
Mrs. Toddy starts the song and gently turns the page.
Her parents hearts are beating hard, their hands reach out and touch.
A tear runs briefly down Mom's cheek as everyone is hushed.

The lights dim slowly on the scene of Mary and the Christ.
The spotlight hits her royal blue that cost them quite a price.
The choir behind her folds their hands and doesn't make a sound.
The introduction fades away as she surveys the crowd.

There's Mr. Bimble, Pastor Glenn, and Sister Mary Jo,
Her family from young to old sits watching in one row.
Then catching glimpse of all the rest, she looks down to the floor.
She can't remember her first line, or second, third or fourth!

The entrance is now long far by, she's staring at her feet.
This awkward pause is making the crowd wiggle in their seats.
The thing most feared has come to pass; can God forgive her now?
She wishes she could scream out loud, "I wish I were a cow!"

When all seems hopeless for the play and our young vocalist,
The music stops and from offstage she hears a gentle "psst."
There Mrs. Toddy sends a smile to calm the girl's great fear.
She comes to her and draws her close to whisper in her ear,

"We'll try again, now, it's OK, just take a nice big breath
And look at Baby Jesus, dear, He'll help you do the rest.
In our weakness He is strong and helps us run the race.
That's why we put this pageant on, so all will know God's grace."

Resuming posture, Mrs. Toddy waves her white baton.
The music starts to play again, as if from heaven beyond.
Sally looks at Jesus' face, her frown turns to a smile,
And with a clear strong voice she sings these lyrics to her child.

"Oh Jesus, precious Jesus, you have come to save us all.
Thank you, my sweet Jesus, you're the greatest gift of all!"

Christmas Plays

Mary and the Christ Child
by Martha S. Campbell

Running Time: 30 minutes

Cast:
- Mary
- Gabriel
- Joseph
- Innkeeper
- Angel Voice
- Shepherd Voice
- Leader—adult
- Scripture Reader—adult
- Poem Reader—adult
- Primary Angels and Shepherds
- Kindergarten Choir

Production Note: Choir music or other special music may be added if a longer program is desired. Costumes may be simple as well as the props. The production is done in four scenes with a service opening.

Prelude: "O Come, All Ye Faithful"

Leader: Come, let us sing the praise
    Of Jesus our King
    Who came to earth;
    Of His wondrous birth
    Both people and angels sing.

Congregational song: "Joy to the World"

Leader *(prayer):* O God, we thank Thee for Christmas.
    We thank Thee for the Christ Child.
    Prepare our hearts for His coming.
    May His coming bring joy to our lives.
    May His coming bring peace to our lives.

May His coming bring love to our lives.
And may we, in turn, give joy, peace, and love to others.

Scene 1

(MARY *is seated on a stool, with a low vase of summer flowers nearby to represent a summer garden. She wears a pastel or flowered dress.* GABRIEL *wears a flowing, white robe and shining headdress.*)

SCRIPTURE READER: "And in the sixth month the angel Gabriel was sent from God unto a city of Galilee, named Nazareth, to a virgin espoused to a man whose name was Joseph, of the house of David; and the virgin's name *was* Mary. And the angel came in unto her, and said, Hail, *thou that art* highly favoured, the Lord *is* with thee: blessed *art* thou among women." (Luke 1:26-28 KJV)

POEM READER: Flowers are all a-blooming,
   Little birds do sing,
   Mary's in the garden
   Mid the flowers of spring. *(Enter* GABRIEL.*)*
   Comes a shining angel
   There beneath the tree.

GABRIEL: "Mary, happy shalt thou be.
   Thou shalt have a baby,
   Gentle, strong and mild;
   God the Father giveth
   Unto thee a child."

MARY: "Great the joy you bring!
   Unto God the Father
   Joyfully I sing."

(*Exit* GABRIEL.)

POEM READER: Mary sings in springtime,
   Sings in summer sun,
   Waiting for the winter
   When the Babe shall come.

(MARY *stands or sits in an attitude of prayer while voice offstage sings "Fairest Lord Jesus."*)

Scene 2

(*Begins after the playing of the previous song . . . used as a brief interlude.* MARY *is dressed in a blue dress with a dark cape or shawl.* JOSEPH *and the*

INNKEEPER *wear dark cloaks.)*

SCRIPTURE READER: "And it came to pass in those days, that there went out a decree from Caesar Augustus, that all the world should be taxed. (*And* this taxing was first made when Cyrenius was governor of Syria.) And all went to be taxed, every one into his own city. And Joseph also went up from Galilee, out of the city of Nazareth, into Judaea, unto the city of David, which is called Bethlehem; (because he was of the house and lineage of David:) to be taxed with Mary his espoused wife, being great with child." (Luke 2:1-5 KJV)

(JOSEPH *and* MARY *enter from far SL.)*

POEM READER: Mary's husband, Joseph,
  Says upon a day:

JOSEPH: "We must go on a journey
  Far and far away."

POEM READER: Mary rides a donkey; (MARY *and* JOSEPH *move slowly across stage.)*
  Joseph walks beside;
  Over hill and valley
  To Bethlehem they ride.
  All the town is crowded,
  Many people shout; *(loud talking heard offstage)*
  Roads are full of donkeys;
  Camels all about.
  Crowded, too, the inn is. (INNKEEPER *enters SR.)*

JOSEPH: "Pray you, sir, a bed!"

POEM READER: Joseph asks for Mary
  A place to lay her head.

INNKEEPER: "No rooms left tonight, sir;
  You must go below;
  Fresh clean stalls for cattle
  There, to you, I'll show."

Instrumental music: "O Little Town of Bethlehem"

Scene 3

(MARY *is seated on a stool by a low manger containing the "Christ Child."* JOSEPH *stands behind her to the left; tableau is CS. A spotlight on the Holy Family and a star overhead would enhance the effect.)*

SCRIPTURE READER: "And so it was, that, while they were there, the days were accomplished that she should be delivered. And she brought forth her firstborn son, and wrapped him in swaddling clothes, and laid him in a manger; because there was no room for them in the inn." (Luke 2:6-7 KJV)

POEM READER: In the stable, Mary
  Lies at close of day;
  Cows are gently lowing,
  Camels chew the hay.
  There that night to Mary
  Is the Christ Child born; *(increase brightness of lights)*
  Soon will bells be ringing
  For the Christmas morn.
  Joseph watches by her
  While the Babe they greet;
  Lay Him in a manger
  Where the cattle eat.
  Donkeys look in wonder,
  Camels ope' their eyes,
  Cows behold the Baby
  In a slow surprise.

KINDERGARTEN CHOIR: "Away in a Manger"

Scene 4

(Primary children representing ANGELS and SHEPHERDS gather at SR; some of the SHEPHERDS are kneeling.)

SCRIPTURE READER: "And there were in the same country shepherds abiding in the field, keeping watch over their flock by night. And, lo, the angel of the Lord came upon them, and the glory of the Lord shone round about them: and they were sore afraid. And the angel said unto them, Fear not: for, behold, I bring you good tidings of great joy, which shall be to all people. For unto you is born this day in the city of David a Saviour, which is Christ the Lord. And this *shall* be a sign unto you; Ye shall find the babe wrapped in swaddling clothes, lying in a manger. And suddenly there was with the angel a multitude of the heavenly host praising God, and saying, Glory to God in the highest, and on earth peace, good will toward men." (Luke 2:8-14 KJV)

POEM READER: Shepherds on the hillside,
  Watching flocks by night,

> See a light a-shining,
> Shining through the night.
> Far away, the shepherds
> Hear an angel sing.

ANGEL VOICE: "Now is born the Christ Child!
> Joy to earth I bring."

ANGELS: "Unto God be glory!
> Peace, good will to all!
> Joy the Christ Child bringeth!
> Now is come to earth
> Life and love and goodness
> With the Christ Child's birth!"

SHEPHERDS/ANGELS (*singing*): "Hark! The Herald Angels Sing"

(ANGELS *exit.*)

SCRIPTURE READER: "And they came with haste, and found Mary, and Joseph, and the babe lying in a manger." (Luke 2:16 KJV)

(SHEPHERDS *move to gather around the manger.*)

SHEPHERD VOICE: Come now,
> Let us seek the Child;
> Find the manger bed.

POEM READER: Shepherds seek the manger,
> Find the Baby there.
> Find the Babe with Mary,
> Mary Mother fair.

> Joseph stands beside her;
> Donkeys stand there too;
> Little lambs are looking;
> Cows are crying, "Moo!"
> Shepherds kneel in wonder,
> Shepherds bow their heads.

SHEPHERD VOICE: "O, be glad, ye people."

POEM READER: So the shepherds say,
> Lo, is born the Christ Child
> Unto earth today!

SCRIPTURE READER: "And when they had seen *it*, they made known abroad the saying which was told them concerning this child. And all they that heard *it* wondered at those things which were told them by the shepherds. But Mary kept all these things, and pondered *them* in her heart. And the shepherds returned, glorifying and praising God for all the things that they had heard and seen, as it was told unto them." (Luke 2:17-20 KJV)

POEM READER: Then they leave the manger,
    Wandering to and fro, (SHEPHERDS *exit.*)
    Telling the happy tidings
    Everywhere they go.

(Enter KINDERGARTEN CHOIR *around the manger.)*
    Many hear the message,
    Come from far and near;
    All the little children,
    To see the Baby dear.

(All cast enter.)

ALL *(singing):* "Go, Tell It on the Mountain" *(Soloist may sing verses with the cast joining on the refrain.)*

(Program LEADER *may speak closing remarks.)*

Congregational Song: "Silent Night"

Benediction

Conversations with Gabriella
by Patricia Souder

Cast:
>GABRIEL—a large angel with deep voice who has lots of presence
>GABRIELLA—a smaller, younger angel with enthusiastic but flighty personality

Props:
>Gabriel—a different colored scroll for each sketch. Scripts can be copied and taped inside scrolls made from Christmas foils or holographic paper. Tie with contrasting Christmas ribbons. Suggested order of colors: gold, green, silver, red.
>
>>For Sketch 2—Earth Time Calculator: cover a box (approximately 8" x 10" x 2") with black paper. Write "Earth Time Calculator" in large letters on large white label on front of box.
>>
>>For Sketch 4—Long, festive bugle: Cut X in the bottom of a clear plastic cup. Tape the bottom of the cup to the outside of a long cardboard roll from Christmas foil to form the bell of the bugle. (Diameter of the bottom of the cup and the roll should be the same.) Tape the triangular points created by cutting the X in the bottom of the cup to the inside of the roll. Spray with gold paint. Decorate with Christmas ribbons and star garland at the neck of bugle. Cloth to "polish" bugle.
>
>Gabriella—different music scores for each sketch. Scripts can be copied and glued inside the scores made from card stock and labeled with names of music Gabriella is trying to learn.
>
>>In Sketch 4—Bottle sprayed gold and labeled "Halo Polish"; a cotton ball; a halo

Costumes:
>Gabriel should be impressive in a white robe with generous, flowing sleeves and large filmy flexible wings trimmed in gold or silver garland. He should also have a gold or silver halo.
>Gabriella should be somewhat less impressive with smaller wings so she looks like an emerging, novice angel. She also has a halo which she can take off and polish in Sketch 4.

Scenery:
>Create the illusion of being high in the heavenly realms by designing

a dark blue backdrop with tiny stars bordered by fluffy white clouds at the bottom
- Cover the platform with white to look like clouds
- Drape a podium with a rich fabric of purple, silver, or gold for Gabriel
- Drape a music stand with a simpler but complementary fabric for Gabriella
- Drape two stools, one higher for Gabriel if possible, with white to give the appearance of being in the clouds

Production Note: These are four angelic sketches in two voices, Gabriel and Gabriella. You might present the individual sketches during the Sundays in Advent; stage all four sketches to create a delightful outreach event; or combine the sketches with choral and instrumental numbers for an unforgettable service of drama and music.

Gabriel's Secret Mission

Sketch 1

Setting: Heaven

Time Period: 15 months before the birth of Christ

(Suggested music: violin, piano, flute or harp playing "Of the Father's Love Begotten")

GABRIELLA	GABRIEL
	(Enters SR carrying a gold foil scroll. Places scroll on podium, sits on stool. Studies scroll until disturbed by GABRIELLA's singing.)
(Enters SL with music score in hand. Tries to sing tune for "Of the Father's Love Begotten." Very off-key.) La...la...la...la...la...la...la	
	(Rolls eyes, clears throat, and sings melody correctly) La...la...la...la...la...la...la...
(Looks up, a bit sheepishly)	
	(Indicates GABRIELLA should sing along.)

(Joins GABRIEL. *Uncertain at first, but gets tuned up and gains confidence by third time.)*
La...la...la...la...la...la...la...la...   *   La...la...la...la...la...la...la...la...
La...la...la...la...la...la...la...la...   *   La...la...la...la...la...la...la...la...
La...la...la...la...la...la...la...la...   *   La...la...la...la...la...la...la...la...
                                                            Good . . . good . . . very good.

(Beams happily. Sings alone)
La...la...la...la...la...la...la...la...la
(Takes deep breath and puts music on stand)
Oh, Gabriel, that's so much better!

                                     (Gabriel nods, then studies scroll again.) Now, let's see . . .
                                     I'm to go to . . .

(Approaches GABRIEL, *tapping him on shoulder)*
Gabriel, why weren't you at choir rehearsal?
You have such a magnificent voice . . .

                                     (Looks up briefly. Smiles)

Besides, we're practicing *the* most *divine* music ever.

                                     I'm sure you are.
                                     (Smiles warmly)
                                     And . . . I love to sing.

Well then, where were you tonight?

                                     (Clears throat and points to scroll)
                                     I have to prepare for a special mission.

(Mouth drops open and eyes bulge. Paces across stage.)
A special mission?
No way!
I'll bet it's a secret mission.

                                     Well, sort of secret . . .

(Rolls eyes)
Sort of secret?
Whoa . . . that's more secret than just plain secret.

> No . . No . . . It's not *more* secret. It's just that nobody knows about it yet.

(Becomes breathless with excitement)
No way!
Nobody knows about it!
Sounds pretty secret to me!

> (Sighs and shakes head)
> Only until I do what the Mighty One has asked me to do.
> (Attempts to study scroll again)

The Mighty One?
You're on a secret mission for the Mighty One?
(Gasps)
Oh, Gabriel, I'm *so* excited I can hardly stand it!
(Gets puzzled look on face and scratches head)
What are you going to do?

> (Looks up, then points to scroll)
> First I have to find a priest named Zechariah.

How are you going to do that?

> (Checks scroll)
> This says that Zechariah will be the priest burning incense in the temple that day.

(Rolls eyes, clasps and unclasps hands)
Oh, Gabriel . . . a temple job!
How exciting!
(Leans forward to ask)
What are you going to tell him?

                                (Checks scroll again)
                                Not to be afraid.

Not to be afraid?
Why would he be afraid?
Do you have a scary message?

                                (Moves finger down scroll as if reading)
                                No, not really. In fact, it looks like it's an answer to a prayer he and his wife prayed for many years.

All right!
(Gestures enthusiastically, then gets a puzzled look)
Then why do you have to tell him not to be afraid?

                                (Stands and faces GABRIELLA.)
                                Well, this will probably sound funny to you . . . but earthlings get pretty frightened when they meet an angel.

Why? Angels aren't scary.

                                Not to us. But earthlings can't usually see us, so it's a bit unnerving when we appear.

Even when we're answering prayers?

                                Even then. *(Pauses and shakes head)* I'd guess Zechariah's going to be very surprised. First, because he's never met an angel before . . .
                                And second, because he stopped expecting an answer to this prayer many years ago.

Oh . . .
(Looks confused)
So why's it being answered now?

(Smiles and points upward)
Gabriella . . .

(Smiles weakly. Speaks hesitantly.)
I guess the Mighty One knows what's best, doesn't He?

(Nods)

So what's the deal? What's going to happen?

Zechariah and his wife are going to have a baby.

A baby?
(Smiles broadly, then exclaims)
No way!

That's what they're going to think.

(Looks confused again)
What do you mean? You said they prayed for a baby. And now they're getting one. They should be happy.

Oh, I'm sure they'll be happy. It's just that they'll be a bit shocked at first.
It's virtually impossible for them to have a baby, you know.

What do you mean?
(More confused then ever)

They're way too old.

Too old?

Yes, too old. Earthlings aren't like us. As the years go by, their skin wrinkles, their joints creak, they can't see, they can't hear . . . and they can't have babies.

(Backs away, rolls eyes, and looks very perplexed)
Well, if they can't have a baby,

why are you going to tell them
that they are?

> I'm just doing . . . *(points up)*

(Nods, rolls eyes, looks up)
what the Mighty One wants.

> what the Mighty One wants.

(Looks at GABRIEL.*)*
Pleasing the Mighty One is important
to you, isn't it?

> *(Nods and smiles warmly)*
> More important than anything,
> Gabriella.

(Takes deep breath; sighs)
Even when you can't figure out why?

> *Especially* when I can't figure out
> why.

(Looks confused)
What?

> It's not what. It's Who.
> *(Smiles knowingly and points up-*
> *ward with a loving look)*

(Watches GABRIEL *closely, then bows*
head.)
You really trust the Mighty One,
don't you?

> He's worth trusting, Gabriella.

(Looks at GABRIEL *and smiles.)*
OK, so when do you leave on
your top-secret, surprise mission?

> *(Peers out into space)*
> Just about now.

Do you think you'll get back in time
for our next rehearsal?

> I'll do my best.

(Picks up music and exits SL, singing
tune to "Of the Father's Love Begotten"
slightly off-key.)

> *(Shakes head, rolls eyes, tucks scroll*
> *under arm, and sings with* GABRIEL-
> LA *as follows* her off SL.*)*

La...la...la...la...la...la...la...la... * La...la...la...la...la...la...la...la...

Suggested music: Group of soloist sings verses 1, 2 of "Of the Father's Love Begotten"

Scene 2

Setting: Heaven

Time Period: 9 months before the birth of Christ

Suggested music: Group or soloist sings verses 1, 2 of "Of the Father's Love Begotten"

GABRIELLA

GABRIEL

(Enters SL carrying music score; struggles to sing last line of "Of the Father's Love Begotten")
Ev-er-more . . .
And ev-er-more . . . .

(Enters SR carrying green foil scroll and Earth Time Calculator)

(Stops singing, notices GABRIEL.)
Gabriel! Where were you tonight? Choir's just not the same without you.

(Smiles and shrugs. Opens scroll and begins to study it as GABRIELLA talks.)

I see you have another scroll.
(Crouches down with inquisitive look)
Does that mean you're going on another secret mission?

Well, sort of.

(Becomes very excited)
Oh, wow! Is it about another baby?

As a matter of fact, it is.

No way!

That's what you said last time.

It's just an expression.

Whatever. All I know is that

No w . . .
(Starts to say "way" but covers mouth quickly and shakes head back and forth. Eyes get big.)
I'm sorry. I didn't mean it. Really. I mean, I can't imagine what it would be like to not be able to talk.

Will he ever be able to talk again?

(Sighs and smiles)
Oh, good!
(Pauses, then asks hesitantly)
How long will that be?

No wa . . .
(Starts to say "way" again but covers mouth quickly and shakes head back and forth frantically. Looks horrified.)
I mean, that's a looong time to not be able to talk, isn't it?

(Nods head, yes)
Glad it's not me!

Zechariah said something like that . . . and he hasn't been able to speak since.

(Smiles and raises eyebrows)
I'm sure you can't!

After the baby's born.

(Holds up Earth Time Calculator and punches in data)
Well, let's see. It's been six months since I gave him the news. Subtract that from the normal nine-months gestational period for earthlings and he has just over three months left.

(Smiles, puts Calculator away)
Pretty long.

(Chuckles)
The silence would stagger the universe.

(Turns away as if offended)
Gabriel!

(Takes deep breath and sighs softly)
Gabriella, I'm sorry. I didn't mean to offend you.
(Goes to GABRIELLA and tries to get her to look at him.)
Why, I'd be real lonely if you weren't here to chatter away.

(Starts to respond, then turns away again when GABRIEL says, "chatter away.")

Gabriella . . . Look, I'm sorry.
(Beat)
Not being able to talk is tough.
(Beat)
Even for Zechariah, *(beat . . . beat)* and he never was much of a talker.
(Looks at GABRIELLA, hoping she'll forgive him.)

(Remains aloof)

(Looks up; lifts hands in prayer)
Um . . . Mighty One . . . this silence treatment . . . *(beat)*
It's pretty hard on all of us. *(Beat)*
I hope you're giving Elizabeth special grace. *(Beat)*
And Zechariah . . . *(beat . . . beat)*
Please give him patience . . .
(beat)
And faith to enjoy the miracles he's about to witness.

(Eyes light up. Turns back to GABRIEL, excited.)
Miracles? I love miracles!

(Sighs with relief, looks up and whispers "Thank You!" Then looks at Gabriella.*)* Gabriella, it's good to hear you talk again!

(Nods grudgingly to Gabriel.*)*
And it's good to hear you say so, Archangel.
(Becomes excited again)
Now tell me about the miracles.

(Looks at watch)
Oh dear, I don't have much time.
(Consults scroll)
I'm to go to Nazareth to tell a young woman named Mary that she's going to have a baby.

(Thrilled)
Another baby mission!
That's so sweet!

(Clears throat nervously)
Yes, well . . . I hope she'll feel that way.

Why wouldn't she? Babies are adorable!

Yes, they are.

So what's the problem?

Mary's not married.

Not the first time that's happened.

But Mary's a virtuous young woman who's a virgin.

Oh . . . I see.

(Furrows brow as studies scroll again)

(Pauses, then looks at Gabriel *with puzzled look.)*
Actually, no, I don't see. I'm not too good on earthling terminology,

but I think there's a problem with "virtuous," "virgin," and "baby" all being packaged together by an angelic announcement.

> Good point. And that's probably what the earthlings will think too.

Like who?

> Oh . . .
> The townspeople . . .
> The religious leaders . . .
> Mary's relatives . . .
> And, *(beat . . . beat)* most importantly,
> *(Beat . . . beat)* Joseph, her fiancé.

Her fiance?
Wouldn't he be likely to know what's going on . . . especially if Mary has any virtue at all?

> *(Consults scroll carefully, shaking head thoughtfully)*
> Well . . . in this case, no.

(Looks perplexed; rolls eyes)
Gabriel, you're not making any sense!
(Lowers voice and shakes head)
I knew those dusty, musty earth vapors
(Wrinkles nose and makes a face)
you brought back with you would get to you!
(Goes to GABRIEL, *pats him on shoulder, and shakes head sadly.)*

> *(Takes deep breath; sighs)*
> Gabriella . . .

(Backs off and lifts right index finger to scold)
No, Gabriel, you listen to me.

This sounds like a seedy case for you, the great archangel, to be involved in.

> Gabriella . . .
> *(Points to scroll, then points up)*
> What's happening is a miracle.
> It's never happened before . . .
> And it will never happen again.

(Drops finger and combative stance)
Oh . . .
Well, why didn't you say so?

> *(Rolls eyes; takes deep breath)*

(Shrugs and smiles sheepishly)
I guess I forgot about the miracle part.
So, what's the deal?

> The Spirit of the Mighty One is going to visit Mary in a special way so she'll become pregnant with the Mighty One's Son.

No wa . . .
(Catches herself and places hand over her mouth.)
I mean, Wow! That's awesome!

> *(Smiles broadly and nods in agreement)*
> Yes, it is.
> *(Looks out over horizon suddenly and re-rolls scroll rapidly.)*
> Hey, I've got to get going or I won't get through the ozone layers in time.
> *(Jumps off stool and rushes to exit SR)*

(Follows GABRIEL shouting . . .)
Wait, I need you to help me with my music!

> *(Turns back briefly and sings)*
> Ev-er-more . . .
> *(Gestures for GABRIELLA to join in.)*

(Joins in midway)
And ev-er-more . . .   *   And ev-er-more . . .
                                              Right on!
                                              (Exits, then peeks back in to say)
                                              Keep practicing!

(Sings and skips happily as exits SL)

Suggested music: Repeat last "Evermore and evermore" and segue to the chorus of "Angels We Have Heard on High"

Scene 3

Setting: Heaven

Time Period: 6 months before the birth of Christ

Suggested music: Repeat last "Evermore and evermore" and segue to the chorus of "Angels We Have Heard on High"

GABRIELLA   GABRIEL

(Enters SL carrying music score and singing chorus of "Angels We Have Heard on High")
"Glo- *(takes breath)* ho-ho-ho-ho-ho . . .
(takes breath) ho-ho-ho-ho-ho . . .
(takes breath) ho-ho-ho-ho-ho . . .
(takes breath) ho-ri-hah!"
Oh dear, I don't think that's quite right.
(Shakes head in discouragement)

                                         (Enters SR carrying silver scroll and singing the first line of the chorus of "Angels We Have Heard on High." Sings with good diction and proper breathing in a strong, resonant voice.)
                                         "Glo————ri—a . . ."

(Runs to meet GABRIEL.)
Why, that's what I was just singing!

                                         Wonderful!

Thanks! I didn't realize I sounded so good.

(Smiles happily, then looks puzzled)
In fact, I didn't even know you heard me.

    I didn't. But I'm glad to hear you're still singing.

Oh. *(Looks a little disappointed, then wistful)*
Do you think we could practice like last time?

    Maybe. *(Holds up scroll)*
    But first, I've got to read up on my next mission.

Don't tell me you have another secret baby mission!

    (Laughs, then offers GABRIELLA *the scroll.)*
    See for yourself.

(Looks at scroll briefly, then hands it back to GABRIEL.*)*
I don't feel like reading. Just tell me what's going on. Did that old couple . . .

    You mean Zechariah and Elizabeth?

(Nods)
Did they have their baby?

    (Smiles broadly)
    They had a big, healthy, robust, baby boy.

So is . . . is . . . Zechariah able to . . . to . . .

    (Laughs)
    To speak again? Sure is. When it came time to name the baby, the townspeople assumed the baby would be named after his father,

which is the custom. But Zechariah got a tablet and wrote, "His name is John," just like the Mighty One told him to do. And when he did, he got his voice back and began praising the Mighty One.

I'm so glad! Now, let's see . . . What about the girl?
(Looks puzzled as tries to remember her name.)

You mean, Mary?

(Nods)
Yes, Mary. Was Mary happy about the miracle baby?

She was surprised. She asked how it would happen since she's never slept with a man. When I explained that the Spirit of the Mighty One would come upon her in a special way, she said, "I'm the Lord's servant. Whatever He wants is fine with me."
(Shakes head in disbelief)
So sweet and simple. No arguments. No complaints. No deals. No demands for signs. Even though it will totally change her life.
(Takes handkerchief out of pocket and wipes a tear from his eye.)

(Looks at Gabriel *quizzically.)* She must really love the Mighty One, huh?

(Nods head)
For sure.

So, how long does Mary have to wait for her baby?

Will she . . . *(takes deep breath and rolls eyes while deciding how to ask question)* Will she *(beat)* be able to speak?

The usual time: nine months.

(Laughs heartily)
Not a problem for Mary. She believed . . . and accepted . . . everything the Mighty One told her.

Well, that's good. *(Beat)* So what's she doing now?

(Stands on tiptoe and peers over edge of stage)
Looks like she's just coming home after visiting Zechariah and Elizabeth for three months.

(Perky)
Well, it sounds like everything's going great.
So why do you have to go on another mission?

(Offers GABRIELLA *the scroll again.)*
Feel free to read all about it.

(Shakes head, no)
No, thanks. I don't think you should have to go to that little dust-ball called Earth again. It's so . . . so . . . small and dirty . . . and you always come back smelling so . . . so . . . earthy. *(Wrinkles nose and makes face)* It's so much nicer here! *(Takes deep breath and throws arms up joyously, as if to embrace the universe.)*

(Clears throat and nods dubiously)
Well, perhaps you should ask for an audience to advise the Mighty One . . .

(Looks at Gabriel in disbelief.)
Gabriel, you know the Mighty One doesn't need my advice!

> Precisely.

Oops. *(Hangs head and smiles weakly)* I guess the Mighty One knows what He's doing, doesn't He?

> *(Nods)*

OK, so what's the scoop this time?

> Remember Joseph, Mary's fiancé?

(Nods head; thinks for a few seconds.)
Oh . . . he doesn't know what's going on, does he?

> *(Shakes head, no.)*
> All he knows is that Mary's pregnant . . . and he's not the father. The law says he can have Mary stoned. He doesn't want to do that, but he can't just pretend everything's all right, either.

Can't Mary explain things to him?

> She could try. But remember, this is a miracle pregnancy. Nothing like this has ever happened before. Mary may feel it's so sacred she shouldn't talk about it. Or she may fear that Joseph will question her honesty . . . or her sanity.

(Looks troubled)
Oh . . .

> Besides, if Joseph believes Mary is really carrying the Mighty One's Son, he may think he no longer has the right to marry her.

(Shakes head sympathetically)

So, you're supposed to tell Joseph what's going on?	
	(Nods) Tonight. While he's sleeping.
(Nods) OK. So how soon do you have to go?	
	(Peers over horizon) About now . . . while I can slip through the thermosphere and slide through the ionosphere without disturbing the mesosphere.
Whatever . . . *(Looks real confused)* But what about practicing?	
	(Chuckles and beckons to GABRIELLA *to come along.)* Let's do it on the way.
Glo . . . . ria . . .	Glo . . . . ria . . .
In excelsis Deo . . .	In excelsis Deo . . .
(Exits SR, singing joyously)	*(Exits SR, singing joyously)*

Suggested music: Showy version of verse 1 and chorus of "Angels We Have Heard on High"

Sketch 4

Setting: Heaven

Time Period: Just before birth of Christ

Suggested music: Showy version of verse 1 and chorus of "Angels We Have Heard on High"

GABRIELLA	GABRIEL
	(Enters SR carrying scroll and long bugle adorned with streamers. Places scroll on podium, then sits on stool and begins polishing bugle with soft cloth.)
*(Enters SL, carrying halo and bottle of halo polish. Sings heartily on key and	

with good tone quality.)
"Glo . . . . ria . . .
(from the chorus of "Angels We Have Heard on High." Self-absorbed at first, but then notices GABRIEL *and stops singing.)*
Oh, Gabriel! I'm so glad you're here. I was worried when you missed practice again because Maestro said it's time for the concert. And we're so ready! Why, we've been practicing our Glorias and Alleluias for eons, and today, they sounded absolutely phenomenal! Every note was perfect! The harmony was heavenly!

(Smiles and nods)
Good!

Gabriel, I know this sounds crazy, but I think the stars were singing along.

(Smiles again, broader this time)
Could be, Gabriella.

(Notices GABRIEL'S *bugle.)*
Hey, what's that you're polishing?

A bugle.

(Adopts playful, mysterious tone)
Yes, but why?

To get the earthlings' attention.

(Distressed)
The earthlings' attention?
(Notices scroll on table, goes over and picks it up)
Don't tell me you have to go on another secret mission!

If I remember correctly, you were very excited the first time I said I was going on a special mission.

Yes, but I didn't know you'd go

so often . . . or bring back such
earthy odors.
(Wrinkles nose)
And now . . . *(Looks troubled)*
If you go now, you're going to miss
the greatest concert ever.

                        (Smiles mysteriously)
                        Do you think so?

Why, yes, of course. The concert's
tonight! We're to make sure our
wings are groomed,
*(inspects wings and makes a few
finger curls)*
our robes glisten,
(brushes and then smooths robe)
and our halos sparkle.
*(Pours some halo polish on a large cotton
ball and polishes halo)*
We're to meet at the tail end of the Big
Dipper for final instructions just as the
shooting stars begin their festivities.

                        (Holds up bugle to inspect it)
                        Sounds good to me.

(Petulantly)
But if you're off on an earth mission,
you'll miss everything.

                        Really?

(Nods vigorously)

                        Did the Maestro tell you why
                        you're meeting at the end of the
                        Big Dipper?

No.

                        Did he tell you where the concert
                        is?

(Looks perplexed)
Well . . . no . . . not really.

> Do you remember any of the words to the songs you've been practicing?

(Perks up)
Oh, sure. Like I told you before, we're singing glorious Glorias and awesome Alleluias in incredible arrangements. It's fabulous music. FAB-U-LOUS!

> *(Smiles mysteriously, polishes bugle a little more)*
> I couldn't agree more.
> But I think you have other words to sing besides Gloria and Alleluia.

(Puts halo on head and thinks hard. Sings to self softly.)
Gloria . . . Gloria . . . glory to God in the highest . . . And peace on earth . . . *(Looks bewildered)* Peace on EARTH . . . *(Eyes grow big)* What on earth does that mean?

> It means harmony and tranquility . . . An inner stillness which grows out of a quiet confidence that the Mighty One . . .

(Rolls eyes)
I know what *peace* means. I live in *heaven*. I just don't think there's any peace on *earth*. So far as I can see, earthlings have been squabbling and bickering ever since they disobeyed the Mighty One in the Garden of Eden.

> True.

So, why are we singing about peace on earth?

                Well, let's see what the master script says . . . "Go to the shepherds in the fields near Bethlehem and tell them: 'Don't be afraid! I bring you good news of great joy for everyone! The Savior has been born tonight in Bethlehem. You'll find Him lying in a manger, wrapped snugly in strips of cloth!'"

(Puts up hands to stop GABRIEL.)
Whoa! Isn't a manger where animals eat?

                (Nods)
                Yes.

Then why would anyone put a newborn baby in a manger? Especially if He's to be a savior of some kind.

                That's a good question, Gabriella.
                (Consults scroll)
                Let's see:
                "Suddenly, the angel will be joined . . ."

(Gasps and covers mouth)
Gabriel, I don't have time to talk about this right now. I've got to get lined up for the concert.

                Whoa, yourself, Gabriella. Listen . . . "Suddenly, the angel will be joined by ranks of angels praising God by saying: 'Glory to God . . . Glory to God in the highest . . . and peace on earth . . .'"
                Now don't those words sound vaguely familiar?

More than vaguely. That's exactly what we've been practicing . . .
(Pauses to puzzle things out)

Hey, wait a minute . . .
Does that mean we're all going with you on this secret mission?

(Nods and smiles warmly)
It's not a secret mission.

Whatever.

We're going to tell everyone . . .

Everyone? *(Eyes get big)*

Everyone who will listen . . . tonight . . . and "ever-more and ever-more."
(Sings to tune from Sketch 1)

No wa . . . *(Covers mouth quickly)*
This is a top se . . . *(Stops abruptly and searches for correct word)*
Top . . . priority mission!
(Checks wings, robe, and halo again. Swallows hard and oozes doubt.)
Ah, Gabriel . . . what's it like to squeeze through gravity?

It takes some adjusting. *(Beat)*

I'm not sure I'll like it.

You'll never know until you try.

I might get my new robe dirty.

You might.

And I'll have to breathe that foul, polluted earth air.

True.

And I'll bet it will hurt when I hurtle through all those layers of the stratosphere.
(Shudders a little)

It can be a little rough.

Then, why are we doing this?

44

(Points to scroll)
Because Jesus is being born in Bethlehem . . .

Jesus? *(Eyes big with disbelief)*
Jesus is being born in Bethlehem . . . ?
(Looks very concerned)
Does that mean Jesus is leaving heaven . . . To become an earthling?

I think that's the plan, Gabriella.

(Overwhelmed)
Why would Jesus do that? Heaven's lonely enough when you're gone, Gabriel.
But Jesus . . . *(beat)*
Jesus is the very heart of heaven. He can't just become a helpless earthling!

(Consults scroll)
It says here that earthlings are at war with the Mighty One because of sin . . . And that the war will never stop until their sin problem is solved because the Mighty One is also the Holy One who cannot tolerate sin in any form.

Like I said: There's no peace on earth. And the earthlings are out of luck.

(Scans scroll while running finger down the columns. Becomes stunned by what he reads.)
It says here that the Mighty One . . . is sending Jesus to pay the penalty . . . *(Beat)* for the sins of the earthlings . . . And that He'll die . . . *(beat . . . beat . . .)*
On a cross.

Jesus is going to die?
(Wide-eyed with horror)

Why would we sing about that?
That's awful!

                        To us. *(Consults scroll again)*
                        But it's the only solution for the earthlings.

Do they have any idea how awesome Jesus is?

                        Probably not.

Jesus spoke the worlds into existence.
And Jesus keeps the universe humming.
Surely there must be some other way
to rescue the earthlings!

                        (Studies scroll again)
                        This says there is no other way, Gabriella. No one else can make them right with the Holy One. No one else can give them peace.

So the Mighty One is sacrificing
His Son . . .

                        (Wipes tear away; clears throat)
                        I think it's called love, Gabriella.

So that's how love works?

                        I guess so.

(Gets tears in eyes)

                        (Looks out over horizon, turns to Gabriella *and extends hand.)*
                        Gabriella, it's time! Are you coming?

(Stands tall; becomes decisive; makes sure halo is on straight)
Why, of course, I'm coming.
The shooting stars are already blitzing through the sky. And . . . *(beat)* after all that practice, I'm sure not going to miss the greatest concert in all of history!

(Exits SL with Gabriel, *singing chorus of "Angels We Have Heard on High.")*

(Blows bugle)
(Exits SL with Gabriella, *singing chorus of "Angels We Have Heard on High.")*

Suggested music: Medley of Christmas carols including
"Angels We Have Heard on High"
"Hark! The Herald Angels Sing"
"O Come, All Ye Faithful"

Secret Service
(Not just a Christmas play)
by Janet Ann Collins

Cast:
>   NARRATOR—if more characters are desired, others could be used for lines spoken offstage
>   CHRIS
>   FRIEND 1
>   FRIEND 2
>   NICHOLAS
>   VILLAGERS:
>>   SOPHIA—a grouchy woman
>>   ROBBIE—a parent
>>   BEGGAR
>>   VILLAGER 1
>>   VILLAGER 2
>>   VILLAGER 3
>>   (More may be used if desired)

Props:
>   3 stools
>   Bible
>   Music stand
>   Red robe
>   Bishop's crown
>   Bouquet of flowers
>   Coat to fit Beggar
>   "Baby" for Robbie to carry

Costumes: All characters wear modern dress throughout except for Bishop's robe and crown. Beggar's clothes should be in poor condition.

Set: The stage is bare except for three stools DSR and a bench USC. You may have a more elaborate set is desired.

Production note: Saint Nicholas was a real person but, since this play is loosely based on legends that have been spreading about him for hundreds of years and not on historical research, there is no guarantee of accuracy.

Scene 1

Time: Present

(NARRATOR *enters and faces audience.*)

NARRATOR: Welcome to our show. *Let us all join in singing, "Oh Come, All Ye Faithful."

(*As audience sings,* CHRIS *wanders out from USR and sits down on stool, facing CS.* CHRIS *yawns and slouches with chin in hands, a picture of boredom. When song is finished,* NARRATOR *exits.* FRIENDS *enter DSL, walking briskly.*)

Chris: Hi.

(FRIENDS *are surprised.*)

FRIEND 1: Hi, Chris! I didn't see you.

CHRIS: I'm sure glad to see you. It's so boring around here.

FRIEND 2: How can you be bored at this time of year? There are so many Christmas activities!

FRIEND 1: Yeah, in just a minute the Christmas program is going to start!

CHRIS: How can you get excited about that? It's the same every year—all about things that happened 'way back in Bible times.

FRIEND 2: You think the Christmas story is boring?

FRIEND 1: God Almighty actually became a baby and you don't think that's anything to get excited about?

CHRIS: Well, I'm a Christian and all that, but you've got to admit, the Christmas story has been told a lot of times. I mean, once your sins are forgiven, what else is there?

(FRIENDS *exchange glances.*)

FRIEND 1: Why don't we all sit here and we'll tell you a story?

(*All sit on stools.*)

FRIEND 2: Once upon a time there was a young man named Nicholas.

CHRIS: I don't remember that Bible story.

FRIEND 1: It isn't a Bible story, but it happened a long time ago. Nicholas lived in Greece and he wanted to go to the far North where he had heard that life was always an exciting adventure. So he took passage on a ship that would start him on his way.

FRIEND 2: But a big storm came up, blew the ship off course, and finally sank it. And then . . . but let's watch and see what happened.

Scene 2

NARRATOR *(lines spoken offstage from this point on)*: The Mediterranean Coast.

(NICHOLAS *enters USR and walks to CS.*)

NICHOLAS: I've been tossed by the waves all night and nearly drowned since the ship sank. I'm cold, wet, and hungry, and I've lost everything I owned except this soggy Bible that washed up on the sand. Now I'll never get to have adventures in the far North. I should have stayed at home in Greece.

Oh well, at least I'm thankful God saved my life. Since I have my Bible, I might as well read it while I rest and wait for my clothes to dry. If I turn the pages carefully, maybe they won't tear.

(*He sits on the bench, shakes the Bible, then opens it slowly, and begins to read silently.*)

NARRATOR: "In those days Caesar Augustus issued a decree that a census should be taken of the entire Roman world. (This was the first census that took place while Quirinius was governor of Syria.) And everyone went to his own town to register.

"So Joseph also went up from the town of Nazareth in Galilee to Judea, to Bethlehem the town of David, because he belonged to the house and line of David. He went there to register with Mary, who was pledged to be married to him and was expecting a child. While they were there, the time came for the baby to be born, and she gave birth to her firstborn, a son. She wrapped him in strips of cloth and placed him in a manger, because there was no room for them in the inn." (Luke 2:1-7 NIV)

CHRIS: I've certainly heard that part of the story before.

FRIEND 1: Shh—he's still reading.

NARRATOR: "And there were shepherds living out in the fields nearby, keeping watch over their flocks at night. An angel of the Lord appeared to them, and the glory of the Lord shone around them, and they were terrified." (Luke 2:8-9 NIV)

FRIEND 2: Wouldn't you have been scared too? (FRIEND 1 *nods.*)

NARRATOR: "But the angel said to them, 'Do not be afraid. I bring you good news of great joy that will be for all the people. Today in the town of David a Savior has been born to you; he is Christ the Lord. This will be a sign to you: You will find a baby wrapped in strips of cloth and lying in a manger.'" (Luke 2:10-12 NIV)

NICHOLAS: When Jesus Christ came into our world He didn't bring any things with Him, either. Maybe God didn't want me to go to the far North. Maybe this is where He wants me to be. Come to think of it, getting shipwrecked and landing in a strange country is a pretty exciting adventure already! OK, God, you're the Lord—the Boss. Please lead me to whatever you want me to do. I'm willing. Amen. (NICHOLAS *listens*.)

    Well, I don't hear any angels telling me what to do, but I think I hear the sounds of a village over that hill. I guess I'll walk to town and see if I can earn a bite to eat.

(NICHOLAS *exits USR*.)

Scene 3

NARRATOR: The Village of Myra.

(NICHOLAS *enters USR and wanders slowly DSC. As he walks, other* VILLAGERS *enter from various places and move around US. Some meet and pantomime greeting each other.* BEGGAR *approaches* NICHOLAS *with outstretched hand.* NICHOLAS *shrugs apologetically. Both keep walking. At CS,* NICHOLAS *meets a group of* VILLAGERS.)

NICHOLAS: Excuse me. I've been shipwrecked and I wonder if you can tell me where I am.

VILLAGER 1: This is the town of Myra in Turkey.

VILLAGER 2: Shipwrecked! You poor thing.

VILLAGER 3: By the way, what's your name?

NICHOLAS: I'm Nicholas, from Greece.

VILLAGER 1: Nicholas!

VILLAGER 2: His name is Nicholas!

VILLAGER 3: Hey everybody, this man is named Nicholas!

(*All* VILLAGERS *gather around and stare at* NICHOLAS.)

NICHOLAS: Hey! What's going on? Why are you all looking at me?

VILLAGER 3: Are you a Christian?

NICHOLAS: Yes . . .

VILLAGER 1: Then you must be the person we've been waiting for!

VILLAGER 2: God told us He would send a man named Nicholas to be in charge of our church.

VILLAGER 3: You've come to fulfill the prophecy.

VILLAGER 2: Are you willing to serve?

NICHOLAS: I asked God to lead me and He brought me here, so that must be what He wants me to do. I'll do my best.

VILLAGERS (*except* SOPHIA): Hooray!

SOPHIA: He's too young to be any good.

VILLAGERS: She's so grouchy! (*To* NICHOLAS.) Come on! We'll show you the church.

(NICHOLAS *and* VILLAGERS *exit USL.*)

Scene 4

CHRIS (*impatiently*): That's a very nice story, but I still don't see what it has to do with Christmas.

FRIEND 1: You haven't heard the good part yet.

FRIEND 2: And it didn't seem very interesting to Nicholas. After a while he found being a bishop was—well, boring.

CHRIS: After the way God led him? If something that exciting happened to me I'd never be bored again. What did he do?

FRIEND 1: Let's watch and find out.

(NICHOLAS, *in robe and crown, with Bible under his arm, enters USL and stands by door of "church" as* VILLAGERS *file out, shake his hand and exit in various places.* SOPHIA *must exit USR after shooing away* BEGGAR, *who has approached her with outstretched palm. A few of the* VILLAGERS *speak as they file past* NICHOLAS.)

VILLAGER 1: Enjoyed your sermon.

VILLAGER 2: Great sermon—thanks.

VILLAGER 3: Nice sermon. We must do something about choir robes.

ROBBIE (*holding baby*): My little baby isn't feeling well. Will you pray for healing?

NICHOLAS: Yes, of course.

(ROBBIE *exits DSR. Other* VILLAGERS *wander offstage except for* BEGGAR, *who looks around for a good place, then lies on floor, DSL, and sleeps. Lights dim.* NICHOLAS *sighs, walks to bench and sits with chin in hands.*)

NICHOLAS: I just don't know what's wrong. I try to serve the Lord as well as I can, but my life is certainly not an adventure. I wish I had gone to the far North instead of staying here. Maybe God didn't really want me here at all and I just misunderstood. But I promised to be Bishop of Myra and I know I should keep my promise.

Lord, please heal Robbie's baby. And I need help too. I thought serving you would be an exciting adventure. Please help me not to be so bored. Amen

(He opens Bible and reads silently as NARRATOR *speaks.)*

NARRATOR: "Be careful not to do your 'acts of righteousness' before men, to be seen by them . . . But when you give to the needy, do not let your left hand know what your right hand is doing, so that your giving may be in secret. Then your Father, who sees what is done in secret, will reward you." (Matt. 6:1-4 KJV)

NICHOLAS: I guess I have been showing off a little bit. It's nice to have people praise my sermons, but there is more to serving God than that. Father, please forgive me and help me to do good secretly. Amen. *(He jumps up and looks around.)* I already see some secrets that need doing! *(He tiptoes off, USL, into church.)*

Scene 5

CHRIS: What's he going to do now?

FRIEND 1: Shh—here he comes.

*(*NICHOLAS' *actions are very secretive. He tiptoes, holds finger to lips, etc., as he enters USL, carrying a coat and flowers. He covers* BEGGAR *with coat.)*

NICHOLAS: That should keep him warm tonight, and with a decent coat maybe he can get a job. (NICHOLAS *tiptoes USR and puts flowers onstage.)* Ever grouchy Sophia will cheer up when she finds beautiful flowers on her doorstep. This is fun! Now I'll go leave some money under the door so Robbie can buy medicine for the baby. *(He tiptoes DSR and pantomimes putting money onstage.)* Nobody will ever guess who did these things! What a wonderful night!

*(*NICHOLAS *dances around with glee, then puts a finger to his lips and tiptoes off USL. As the lights come up,* SOPHIA *enters up right and pantomimes finding flowers, the* BEGGAR *gets up, discovers coat and puts it on.* ROBBIE *enters DSR and finds money. They exit immediately.)*

Scene 6

NARRATOR: Inside the village church.

*(*NICHOLAS *brings music stand to CS, places Bible on it, and stands behind it,*

facing audience. VILLAGERS 1, 2, *and* 3 *enter from various places and stand in a row, slightly DS from* NICHOLAS, *facing CS.* BEGGAR *crosses from USR to join* VILLAGERS.)

BEGGAR: With my new coat I got a job easily. I don't need to be a beggar anymore!

(SOPHIA *crosses from USR and joins* VILLAGERS. *She shows flowers to* NICHOLAS *as she passes him.*)

SOPHIA (*smiling*): See the beautiful flowers? Someone must love me after all! (NICHOLAS *smiles and nods.*)

VILLAGERS: She's not grouchy!

(ROBBIE, *holding baby, enters from DSL and joins* VILLAGERS.)

ROBBIE: Someone gave me enough money to buy medicine. My baby is well now!

NICHOLAS: Let us celebrate the birth of Jesus Christ by praising God!

(*All except CHRIS and FRIENDS sing "Joy to the World," then exit SL. CHRIS and FRIENDS watch and move to CS as others exit.)

Scene 7

CHRIS: Well, that was an exciting story. And I think I'm beginning to understand. Nicholas celebrated the birthday of Christ by living the way Jesus taught. Is that it?

FRIEND 1: Well, not quite. Nicholas didn't stop with Christmas. He made secret giving a way of life, and a wonderful life it was!

FRIEND 2: Whenever the people of Myra needed something they couldn't get for themselves, Nicholas would secretly give it to them if he could. He kept his giving secret until he was an old man with a long, white beard.

FRIEND 1: In fact, it wasn't until after Nicholas died that anybody realized he had been the mysterious helper. Then the people understood the reason for his jolly laughter and the merry twinkle in his eyes. Because he had been such a good Christian, people began to call him "Saint Nicholas."

FRIEND 2: They told everybody about him, and as the years passed, people all over the world heard the story.

FRIEND 1: The name "Saint Nicholas" changed as the story passed from land to land and language to language. In America, we say "Santa Claus," and pretend he lives at the North Pole.

CHRIS: So in a way, he did get to have adventures in the far North.

FRIEND 1: Well, sort of. We know he's really in heaven. But the important thing is that because of Nicholas, people celebrate the birthday of Jesus Christ by giving secretly.

FRIEND 2: And often when they give each other surprises and don't want anyone to know who did it, they say, "It's from Santa Claus!"

CHRIS: So that's what Santa Claus has to do with Christmas! Hey—do you think God would still make life an exciting adventure for Christians who do good things secretly?

FRIENDS: Of course!

CHRIS: It would be so cool to serve God secretly all year, not just at Christmas time. But if I started doing it now, you'd know that it was me. Too bad other people don't do secret good deeds anymore.

FRIEND 1: How do you know they don't?

CHRIS: Do you mean you . . . ?

FRIENDS: Shh!

FRIEND 2: We'll never tell!

CHRIS: Well, if there are already other Christians doing secret service, I could do it without anybody guessing it's me. And if the others happened to figure it out they probably wouldn't tell since we're all doing it for Jesus, right?

FRIENDS: Right!

CHRIS: But I thought we were supposed to tell people about our faith. How can we share it and keep it secret at the same time?

FRIEND 1: That's easy. We tell what He does for us, but we don't tell what we do for others. Now, if you'll excuse me, I have something confidential to take care of. Bye! (FRIEND 1 *exits.*)

FRIEND 2: I need to go too. I have an adventure waiting! See you later. (FRIEND 2 *waves and exits.*)

CHRIS (*smiling*): I won't even try to guess what they're up to. Now I've got to think of a secret good deed I can do myself . . . the first of many.

(CHRIS *crosses to behind music stand and picks up Bible.*)
    Hey! I wonder if there's anything else I never noticed in here

that's as great as this secret service idea. I think I'll check it out. (*Turns pages and seems to read.*) This is exciting stuff! I'll bet if we all really live the way God wants us to, we can turn the world upside down!

(CHRIS *starts to exit DSL, reading while walking.* NARRATOR *enters DSR.*)

NARRATOR: Hey, Chris! (CHRIS *looks up.*) I could use some help. (*Motions for* CHRIS *to join him at CS. To* CHRIS.) Would you like to lead this song?

CHRIS: Well, it's not a secret, but I'd be glad to help wherever I'm needed. (*To audience.*) Let's all sing "Silent Night" together. (*ALL *sing.*)

CHRIS (*at close of song*): Isn't this a wonderful season? Merry Christmas, everybody!

ALL (*from offstage*): Merry Christmas!

(*Exit*)

*Singing may be eliminated or other Christmas music may be chosen if desired.